REFUGIA

REFUGIA

Kyce Bello

UNIVERSITY OF NEVADA PRESS *Reno & Las Vegas*

University of Nevada Press | Reno, Nevada 89557 USA
www.unpress.nevada.edu
Cover art by Aaron Morse
Cover design by Diane McIntosh/Bright Ideas!
Image p 1: © vertyr / Adobe Stock.

LIBRARY OF CONGRESS CATALOGING-IN-PUBLICATION DATA

Names: Bello, Avtar Kyce, 1981– author.
Title: Refugia / Avtar Kyce Bello.
Description: Reno ; Las Vegas : University of Nevada Press, [2019] | "Refugia
  are areas of relatively unaltered climate that are inhabited by plants and
  animals during a period of continental climatic change...and remain as a
  center of relict forms from which a new dispersion and speciation may take
  place after climatic readjustment. Merriam-Webster"—Provided by
  publisher. | Includes bibliographical references. |
Identifiers: LCCN 2019007768 (print) | LCCN 2019009895 (ebook) | ISBN
  9781948908337 (ebook) | ISBN 9781948908344 (pbk. : alk. paper)
Subjects: LCSH: Nature—Poetry. | Climatic changes—Poetry.
Classification: LCC PS3602.E4584 (ebook) | LCC PS3602.E4584 A6 2019 (print) |
  DDC 811/.6—dc23
LC record available at https://lccn.loc.gov/2019007768

The paper used in this book meets the requirements of American National
Standard for Information Sciences—Permanence of Paper for Printed Library
Materials, ANSI/NISO Z39.48-1992 (R2002).

FIRST PRINTING

Manufactured in the United States of America

The earth as it is has always been
is saying its goodbyes.

—Chase Twichell

Refugia are areas of relatively unaltered climate
that are inhabited by plants and animals
during a period of continental climatic change . . .
and remain as a center of relict forms from which
a new dispersion and speciation may take place
after climatic readjustment.

—Merriam-Webster

Contents

PART I

3 Refugia (1)

5 Dear Future Child

7 The Ashram at Leigh Mill Road

8 Guide to Flowering Plants

10 The Trouble with Belief

11 Refugia (2)

12 The Tree Coroners

13 Message in a Bottle from the Sea of Cortez

14 Grail Story

15 Phrases in the Original Unspoken

16 Brief Guide to Epigenetic Memory with Burning Bosque

17 Refugia (3)

19 Paper Trail

21 Equinox

22 Grass Widow

24 In the Air Before Easter

PART II

27 Portrait of the Homemaker at Eighteen

28 I Wear Long Skirts for My Own Unwary Pleasure

29 Refugia (4)

31 Notes for Future Botanists in Search of Conifers

33 The Speaker Reconciles with Spring

35 For the Record

36 Solar Pinholes

39 Gazing on the Midmorning in an Expression of Solidarity

40 Refugia (5)

41   Crossing Elwood Pass

42   The Washerwoman Maps Her Body Before Death

44   The Carp Pond

48   Dowsing

49   Refugia (6)

50   Field Notes

PART III

53   Rinconada

55   Summer Ends with Ringing

56   Landscape with Santa Fe River Restored
            to Its Historic Channel After 100 Years

58   Refugia (7)

59   Fall Reckoning

60   When We Gathered to Stock Up On Light

62   Cusp with Various Visitations

63   Our Names Unfurl Across Winter

67   Refugia (8)

68   Further Phrases in the Original Unspoken

69   Omega

70   Archipelago of Ancestral Bodies and
            Unnamed Landmarks of the Present

79   Refugia (9)

81   Waveform

82   Origin of the Apple

87   Right of First Refugium

89   Acknowledgments

91   Notes

93   About the Author

I

Refugia (1)

The letter came, a white wing.

The envelope opened
        like the sphinx moth
whose careening

        maps the garden's scrawled branches,

or the mourning dove
        in the apple tree who calls

at dawn before lifting
        from her nest.

        Every evening the moth alights

on each blooming weed.
        Every morning, that haunting

cry out the window.

I write back in pine needles, beetle wings,
say, look how far we have flown

in our flaming wreck.

Our trajectory a measure
          of water stress,

tree death a status in three: plant, region, globe.
          My hand in yours.

We have undergone, transpired,
and here we are at collapse—

Though sun reaches our faces

we hold ourselves apart
and name ourselves

after what we survived.

Dear Future Child

The winter the oil dipped
in the barrels and the desert was gridded
for drills and all the new wars began

was like every other except we learned
to sing harmonies as the children slept,

and now and then rain clattered the roof.

He found the notes we needed.
I held the melody lightly between my lips, lightly

as they say to do with questions
and other things that waver in our hands.

On nights we didn't take down our instruments
I wrote a book of letters. Each one began

Dear Future Child.

In the distance between us, invasive roses
make the back passage impassable—

Bars of small leaf and barb.

The letters always end with a bouquet of purple asters that wilt before I can weave them into crowns.

I drive to the market for more flowers

      wishing that driving were already banned
and remember that at night when we sing,

the moment our voices separate is the moment they
    become beautiful.

The Ashram at Leigh Mill Road

Imagine the herbarium I might have made
in childhood. Jewelweed houses

in the seep and furrow.
Paths winnowing verdant darkness.

Before we left those woods,
we gathered every sunrise

to pray and belong to one another.
In the green, dogwood arms of Virginia,

my own name was holy.
When we left, we did not take anything.

My name fettered into freight,
the warm creature of it held.

Every day I wake up and wonder
if I should trouble myself with belief,

and if so, in what. The world green
and long-legged out the window,

runoff guttering to the creek.

Guide to Flowering Plants

The old herbalist smoked Nat Sherman's
           roadside amongst stands of ambrosia

and wild peony, and I would tell you
           what he said, only it was long ago.

Ivey drew eighty pages of *Asteraceae*
           in his guide, but I will never find

the name of these dried yellow petals
           pilfered by felon winds.

           My head covering unravels,
a white flag whipping across white-gray sky.

           It leaves me bereft,
but able to pray with my ears.

           Silence runs through
the house like seams of gold
           mending a cracked *kintsugi*,

           the bowl rendered precious
by its breaking.

A new vessel replaces the fractured one,
now filled.

        Steam canopies
     the room before vanishing.

Thunder barrows over our voices.
There are fields that hold fields that hold fields.

        Blades of grass wind-bent to the ground.

Footfalls between now and the storm's first scattered rain.

The Trouble with Belief

We think we know the best place
to gather chanterelles,

how to sit out lightning bursts
above timberline. I've been waiting

for autumn to start singing,
and meanwhile the ash and elm

have quietly gilded their leaves.
Every time I talk about the trouble with belief,

my friends look away. All I'm saying is
what could it mean that the robes we wear

can be taken off and on?
Or maybe it's simple: trees go

from bare to bud, green leaf to gone
in tides of adornment and scarcity.

We did not find those bright mushrooms
when we scoured the mountain,

only swaths of burnt forest,
only thunder cracking beneath our feet.

Refugia (2)

My face a furrow,
the creek shanks haltered in birdsong.

On the mountain, late winter becomes a cape
fanned open, its seams a congregation of rivulets

ravishing the watershed, then gone.

What is the shape of loss as it robes and disrobes us?

Cars harpoon the roads. Doors slam.
My daughter has a birthday, and all the gifts

I gave but did not name peer back at me
from her arms.

This bed, this meal, these arms.

I task her with tallying drought
as it withers and ferns her fingertips.

Our thirst a palm-sized map etched in broken lines.

Grief leaps from the gorge bridge.
We call it a magpie,

call out as it becomes a flock, as the flock frays in flight.

The Tree Coroners

In laboratories they count tree rings,
graph snowmelt and needle-fall. For decades,
they've watched two degrees determine
by which means a tree will choose to die—
hunger or thirst. The delicate doorway
of each pine needle's mouth hanging open,
or snapped closed. I spend the last hours
of sleep looking over my shoulder, dream
resurrection ferns unfurling in south-
eastern woods. Which boast to believe? My own,
or *their* malediction? Might as well ask
which forest will claim my ashes. The one
I coax into a chase, or the one I run alongside?
The one I walked in before you were born.

Message in a Bottle from the Sea of Cortez

All the gods in mourning, it reads—
        ripple and perennial swell.

The page dressed in brush-stroke estuaries,

the precise place where river turns
to sea in grass and salt flat, tides

that push and pull on the continent's
tucked-in folds, its peninsula, its bay.

There are painters whose pigment
        is allowed to weep,

whose page is allowed its geography
as I am allowed this salted tide.

The mapmaker cries out when riverwater
and seawater become one water,

and the bottle breaks from holding it in.

Grail Story

From the swallowtail morning I take up my list
of whom to forgive.

If you ask me to hammer this engine back to life
        you will hear
how we forged our fool's walk into gold,

        how our fractured bones
were set into ladders spanning a splintered forest,

and we lived for years with the hair raised on the backs of
        our necks.

Beyond the scriptures there is more to give credence
and open-handedly praise.

Please empty this kettle teeming with bones
as if it were a loom and we charged to dress the wound

by asking ten thousand times

        What ails thee?

        Watch how it stills the wind. How it heals
holding knives that open but don't carry us away.

Phrases in the Original Unspoken

I follow the trail until it goes cold,
hunt until my best dogs fail. As they flee,

white-tailed deer abandon silence
for invisibility. I hear them

crest cliffs, disappear between mesquites.
I catch your eye a dozen times. Two sharp

ears look back. We cut limbs
from spruce trees, carry home boughs

wrapped in shawls. Ragged edges
arrange themselves into wreaths,

green hoops I hang on closed doors.
I set garlands upon nails

hammered into my shoulder blades.
They rise and fall as I fly.

Brief Guide to Epigenetic Memory
with Burning Bosque

Bouquet is diminutive for grove, for bosque
gathered up and strummed: Loves me, loves me not.

We say "children of our own" as if the eyes matching ours

did not emerge from body after body arriving
      in the same bloody way—
            knives cutting seeds into swales.

All week, cottonwoods blaze,
      edging the river's scant quicksand in black slashes,
the willow understory fired away.

In the aftermath, I take a turn naming
each of my daughter's small arrivals—

                the gates swinging open
to reveal an overgrown thistle field
where her body takes root and knots off its vine.

      We sigh and agree we look like our mothers—
gazes steady as the river.

When the banks finish burning,
the current carries ash in its rope.

Refugia (3)

It's been June all January. Like the creek,
I've turned to sand.

I empty cisterns onto
trees and bid them not bloom.

Three months ago,
a beaten child was shoved in a shallow grave

near the same river
       where we saw a solitary monarch
skim fringed willows,

its jewel wings flickering
       open and closed

the way my daughter's hand
catches and releases my own.

When the boy's body was found
we began to howl.

Among our laments
were the months it took to discover
he was gone.

Among our options there is creeping north

like moose fleeing ticks,
       and yet I want to stay still

and let this dried-out desolation
be my home all spring.

Paper Trail

I expect my own nest wants tending—the coop in need
of mucking, the uncollected eggs,

the pages I hang on the clothesline to air.

A friend, turning eighty, says, *write for your great-grandchildren,*
who will want to know you, but maybe you don't exist.

My little one tells me she won't be a mother.
She wants horses, and to take care of me.

I'm alone at the breakfast table, drinking tea. The floor
is dusty and scattered in breadcrumbs, in paper scraps.

Last night, the children cut out Valentines. Heart after heart.
It makes such a mess.

I thought I would be barren—
            my cycles parched rivers I recorded 53 times.

53 little windows peeking into the henhouse, and each egg
      a mistranslated word,
their sum a dictionary to a forgotten mother tongue.

Strange how hard it is to speak to the future, to leave a
      paper trail.
What I really want to say is,

learn to roast a chicken properly, and, *walk every day,* but surely
advice is useless to the unborn.

Perhaps I should write what I want to hear from the past:

my grandmother's grandmother sighing in satisfaction
at the sight of me. *You are the best thing that could have
happened next,* she says,

even though I am unbaptized. Even so, she approves.
My children are still children, but already I approve of
their grandchildren.

I want them to know about that day in the high country
when we followed Tesuque Creek until it disappeared
into the mountain.

We found words we couldn't read strewn along the
banks. I gathered them with a knife,

cut them like wild mushrooms from the ground and set
them in my basket.
I turn every last one gently, warm them with my palm,

and whisper, *I thought
I knew your name but I was wrong.*

Equinox

Yes, that is spring hatching between my hands.

Thawed soil, bees in the early-
        blooming apricots.

Every planting season,
worries of drought or calamity

fall silent as cisterns brim
        with the late snows of winter.

What isn't a garden, or a seed slipping into earth?

Inside the open door, a basket
        of unfolded cloth, unswept floors.

                When snow falls in April,
it flutters over plum blossoms.

Light pierces heavy skies.

        Gentleness, open me.
The seeds are beginning to rise.

Grass Widow

Say there is a cleaving that skims
big bluestem into grass-drifted hills,

the dowager's body a-sway
as she harvests nettles,

then trembles toward last light.
In 1871 locusts covered the prairie

with the sound of a million small scissors
snipping green to its knees.

On relict grasslands in Iowa,
milkweed and owl-clover cosset

             untidily into bloom.
Small mammals furrow muck

into trenched seed beds, and I,
I am full of babies.

My breast tunes its small ear
to a particular bawl

drawn from crested ridges.
The land widens, curves, reduces.

There are departures that leave no question
as to who is left behind,

and with how little.

In the Air Before Easter

This town of mine seems ordinary.

                       Only for a few weeks in March
when apricot trees flower on every street

can we begin to understand how much fruit mattered

to the people who built the houses now ours.
Pearl white blooms shading chained dogs, adobe walls.

                       Turn a corner and it is the same
on the next street, the next.

This flowering breath the first wearing away of winter.

I learn the word *caesura* when the canopy's high clamor
falls silent

                       for the longest second
before a single trill
        is answered by ten thousand.

The world whispering,
       soften. Lean back.

       Do not speak a little longer.

II

Portrait of the Homemaker at Eighteen

Behind the sway and gentleness,
I was a weed half grown,
a hatchet ringing against cold.
Our kitchen had mud walls
and one door, globemallow strung
from nails. In winter, dirty windows
filtered sun in streaks. To get out,
we boiled water in the kettle
and poured it real slow on the frozen
runner of the sliding glass door,
and still I don't know why that glass
never cracked. At sundown,
the hills lit up with piñons
glowing like fountains of golden needles.
It must have been one of them
that stitched the dress of light and long shadows
I stepped into as we walked—
dust pouring from the seams.
You'd think that would make any man believe,
but he never could decide to marry me,
though he is still my husband today.
I held his hand as we climbed the ridge
with the day's last light. Held a skillet
and broom. Held my cup of trembled tea,
taken and cut and scalding good.

I Wear Long Skirts for My Own Unwary Pleasure

I wear long skirts for my own unwary pleasure,

look down in photos because my full gaze catches fire
and the floor burned away a thousand houses ago.

I stay busy all day in the reliquary.
So many splinters to shrine in the sun.

So many beads to ply with sweet names
and pass between my fingers.

I will call *this* little piggy God, and *this* little piggy God.

I sing the golden note for my friends,
and ribbon their hair into rope,

take in prisoners but never ask what they have done to be in
   chains.
I do not let them open the door to my cellar.

They shackle and murmur until I feed them apples with a knife,
   slice open star after star after star.

Refugia (4)

Overwintering theories abound

with lessons I will apply
to taming my petulance.

Still, I burn when crossed.

During the last glacial,
fireweed went in pursuit of soil—

long leaves ragged along the same crags
they have rambled over for epochs.

Paleo-pollen indicates shore-pines
walking away from ice

and though I fret over the fate
of fir and piñon,

a biologist with a baby at her breast
says these mountains

were not long ago
populated by different trees altogether.

She says grief
is losing what we know of home,

while the land drifts
into a thousand small harbors,

and leaves us
to our short lives, our quick tempers.

Notes for Future Botanists in Search of Conifers

"Los Alamos National Laboratory study forecasts disappearance of
conifers by end of century due to climate change"
—Santa Fe New Mexican, 2015

The best we can do
                is ignite

and hide
in the forest's open frame.

Perhaps it is blight,
        or age

but I take every red-brown bough
               as rebuke

and cannot bear them

        any easier
than I did my child.

Have you a symbol
            for wooden petals
that spiral into stars?

Have you found
        a new way

to prick your finger?

Blood scratches us
          into tenderness.

If the finished world warms itself
into a midden,

follow this map:

              Limbs sheaved
into green needles.

The wind-awry music

             of branches
undulating overhead,

the owl severing
understory

        to claim its prey.

The Speaker Reconciles with Spring

Here in half spring, elm seeds become first wither
and release, first rain pattern on roof,

first feast we gather by hand.

I imagine the day my daughter will declare
she knows there is no God.

Her eyes a forest of backlit boughs,
        a woodland where I lose my way
despite following the creek.

God, I could tell her, is your knowing,
not the thing you know.

Take the elms the week they unfurl
their glamour of seeds—

tiny green wings that fill each crack
        in the city's palm,
that skitter and cleave into place.

Or how, in the studio, the pietà emerges on paper

only when dark lines of charcoal
render depth and detail. Without shadow

and smudging, God's face cannot bow to us.

Green-tipped trees how winter reveals,
stirs, and lifts the sap.

For the Record

I have often said that *you* refers to him
except for when it means *me.*

Though we see no color ripening
among the leaves, pale yellow apricots

appear on the flagstones each morning.
You insist that they are thrown

over the fence by the child next door,
but she has no fruit tree. And so we go

until we take up smashed fruit, and taste.
We have three ways to see,

said Hugh of Saint Victor, and the hardest eye
to look with is called true sight. I wrestle

with the small mess "you" leave behind,
but do not know if it is his, or mine.

Solar Pinholes

I.
Small fruits and the apple limbs
bend. Each morning the river
lengthens or draws back, a lick of water,
slate of damp sand. Women gather
around bouquets of pink cosmos
to say that before the merciful rain
they were a tangle that could not rise.
In the moth-wing shadow at bedtime
their daughters call for cool cloths,
press them to clavicle and cheek.
What we know of heat is the understory
of summer: waxy-leaved junipers
preserve moisture by not breathing.
Curious waves of light. July and the morning
is a retreat of lilac bushes, shock of gray
sticks between here and—

2.
Midsummer, we wait.

Grasshoppers no longer *chirp*, *chirp*, but sing *chee*, *cheee*.

Who is watching the children?

Spilled ice dissolves into the patio's fluid shadows.

The younger sister dips her head underwater, emerges haloed
    in droplets.

Hollow thud of empty barrels.

A white cat discovers a nest of mice in the woodpile.

The gardener bends and digs turnips, their tops wilted and
    flea-torn.

"I want to do more."

Her eyes are so unlike my own.

Well water on hard, waffled ground.

Crossed fingers. Sun patches between leaves.

3.
Small suns cast from large sun:
light lands in circles on ground.
Heard from another room, speech

is only murmur and pattern.
After a game of making a handful
of pebbles into seven sisters,

the girls notice an orb weaver's web
spun beneath our eaves. The bantam
hen is broody. She will not lift her hot belly

to water or feed. I reach under her
and roll drought-colored eggs, warm,
into my hand. From beneath

a chamisa bramble, the small brown winging
of birds. Midday, the apple tree
dapples shadowed ground in sequins.

Gazing on the Midmorning
in an Expression of Solidarity

Just now I noticed
      my ordinary face

origami into, then upon itself.

      With each new fold,
      the creature of it changes:

         turtle into crane into the way
      my gaze once lifted to yours.

      I pluck grains from the salt
cellar, prepare a feast that tastes of lick and spoil.

         The river ribbons over rock
      in that other tongue

taken up by beaver, oh no, it's not
      a tail slapping water, it's rain

on my roof. It took years
      to become this lovely.

Refugia (5)

2.6 million years of alluvia collect into a new land.

Mountain avens and muskox cross-pollinate, reproduce, and
    persist,
                            until major disturbing events
            alter their ecological trajectory.

After fires one, two, and three, the mountains
            cease to breathe. I love

making love in aspen groves every autumn,
                but of course we are barely a consequence.

Our toes digging into leaf drifts, the water
just out of reach.

The forest succeeds itself in waves
we watch unfold:

pages of *Quercus*, then quaking aspen
rewrite the contoured book

                         and the mountain turns

to something other and unknown,
growing beyond us.

Crossing Elwood Pass

We travel dirt roads that exhaust us
with die-off—every conifer between Platoro
and South Fork shaggy-limbed and gray, snags
mapping the mountain's black lung. The girls
murmur in the backseat, sketching tiny figures
that they arrange into families with torn edges
and lives narrated fluently in verbs. Hear
how they bound, how they comfort, how they cry.
We take oxygen for granted along the creek
where we lay a blanket in bread
and bruise the scent from yarrow with bare feet.
We heard a child was lost that day
in the San Juans, and crossed Elwood Pass
not knowing his fate. No sign of search crews,
but that's just it: no sign, save forty washboard miles
of the forest beckoning its retreat. At timberline
we crouch beneath dead trees to snip
arnica blooms, the yellow sprawl of petals caught
in long shafts of unhampered, unblocked light.

The Washerwoman Maps
Her Body Before Death

I taste flowers by stepping on them.
Flor de Maga on my breath.

I speak hurricane and palm frond,
take in laundry to scrub and hang

like ghosts on a line—

men and women walking, bodiless,
through the tropical night.

On the day a needle enters my palm,
sharp in the folds of laundry,

emerald-beaked birds cry
Boriqua Boriqua Quien Quien Quien?

Every morning at the clinic, X-rays
            track the broken needle-tip
as it rivers upstream,

quicksilver bright against my bones.

Length of arm.
            Bend of shoulder.
The twin wings of my breath.

While I wait for death,
      birds sing their questions to me

and I embroider red buds on the rumors
      my daughter will wear.

The Carp Pond

*

I'm listening for bells, and the sound
of people spilling towards burial,

but all I hear are my children humming
            as they mound sand
on the gouge we call riverbed,

brightly hatted heads bent together
like two nodding tulips.

The sound of spring is so slight,

the water so scant and temporary
its first days are the same as its last.

What does this have to do with death?

I'm just telling a story about what happens
when rivers are held back.

The way willows green, slowly,
            and water flows, barely.

*

One hundred and fifty years ago, springs filled
the carp pond in the Archbishop's garden.

     Behind the cathedral,
in the lot where everyone parked
at this morning's wake,
               the pond
was a golden catch of sunlight,

The river held water, the water held
a wetland, thick with warblers
          and soft-leaved herbs.

I know one young mother who,
like everything else,
         is underground
and gone.

This should be the river singing to you,
but how, I ask, could she?

*

Thirteen people gather to mix the waters
of the world into a bowl.

Here is the Amazon River, here a spring
        on Crete, here
a cupful of our river drawn from the tap
of my kitchen sink.

Summer 1883, the river rose above its banks,
        flooded
the dirt streets of the plaza, dragged
cottonwood logs downstream.

At the archive, I trace the river's dry line
through a folder
        fat with obituaries for its water.

Marshes, trout, floodplains that once spread
        like pearls
on a necklace worn by the woman
dressed in blue,

her song rustling willow, the shuish
        shuish
of a plastic bag caught on a water-
worn branch.

*

The carp pond was hung in willows
whose catkins beckoned bees,

laced in cattails with floating star seeds.

Ponds are where water
        stares back at you,
rising from the dark below.

It's harder to miss a funeral
            than to go.

How else can the world come back to life?

Rise and whir of dragonflies
through the green-fringed door.

How full our wells once were.

Dowsing

Driving from one shady place to the next takes all day,
and if it seems we get along
        I will tell you the frenzy

of locoweed blown flat against the highway's hot river.

At the malpais, we hold hands but cannot speak. Our lips
leafless and barbed as ocotillo.

Near the border crossed by its ten thousandth child

rangers ramble the desert, pierce
        plastic bottles scattered beneath mesquite.

        Traces of water seep from yucca spears and cactus
to the tangled grass

        where each green blade is pressed down
in a bed of green blades.

We cannot sing save for plucking petals

and placing them on the relief of our tongues.
We almost have words for love

only to find they mean hand, they mean
open, they mean
        here was a place to drink.

Refugia (6)

You will want what I want—
some sweet spot canopied in buffered slope.

Each hidden canyon a separate refuge.
Our bodies turn ancient in their retreat,

as in snowshoe hare leaping like a white
flare across brown earth

or the pika nibbling lichen
from alpine talus,

storing yarrow feathers in haystacks
for winter.

You will want like I want.

We will fluctuate our arrivals
into a pattern,
                        count species

on our fingers, follow folded seams
leaking groundwater into pools.

Snatched remnants of the old world crowded
into this refuge,

our houses burned behind us.

Field Notes

If we perish—I meant to say persist—
                do we arise and turn

with the wind? Each leaf slipped
from its bud. Not unlike our first steps

                upon a shady trail, not unlike
an unassumed answer, or the clear space it contains.

                Longing is half the summoning.
In each copse we stumble upon,

      our clothes undone
and thrown
          to tangles of wild geranium,

                  green gentian flowers
cast wide-open eyes upon our skin.

Again and again
          we arrive upon the ground.

                I have drawn it
as true to life as I know how.

III

Rinconada

The orchard is a ramshackle basket
of small feasts gleaned from bent branches,

the untended earth littered in apples,

     as if our origins had been scattered
and left to seed. Perched on ladders,

     our children have round cheeks, wisps
of hair glowing, as the leaves do,

with slanted equinox light.
They reach for peaches, small ones

hung like tiny suns they can taste.
I would take any wreck along this river

and hang my lace in the windows
while the last of the fruit,

     dark maroon and glowing,
spoils with sweetness.

     Somewhere in my recipe box
is the one that returns me to my bearings.

I can't find it, but just remembered

        that to make the best applesauce,
all you need are the best apples.

When was the last time you left something
to cook in its own ravening juices?

Summer Ends with Ringing

I am trying to write my way into a Sabbath,
and won't let this poem leave the house on Saturday
except on foot and wearing a good hat.

I don't want friends anymore, just people
who mail me leaves folded into envelopes,
who send letters wrapped in green

the way a New England forest wraps overhead
like a caul, a rooftop, a breathing, leafy cage.
Maybe it's time to break the waters and see

if there is a clapper in the cracked bell or not.
I call it a bell, this late season when morning glories
carouse the house until they fold petals

and lie still. The sunflowers all dark seedy
hearts, their stalks drooping beneath the small
weight of house finches, so thorough in their hunger.

Landscape with Santa Fe River Restored to Its Historic Channel After 100 Years

Of all my hungers, I like autumn best,
                that murky pond haloed
in lustrous orange,

        cattail spikes softening into fluff
laden spheres,
            the hills thicketed in rumex

and saltbush, both leaves and incendiary seeds
        that hue toward tawny brown,
            then burn in loquacious light.

What if *my* scant waters were let loose
in a direction suggesting home?
            Some long ago uprooting corrected

and beneath my photograph
        a small note
            reading *restored*, like this mottled swill

of leaf and meadow, or the creekbed
        in the Cascades redirected
from a southerly slope to resume

        its original channel to the north—
            a faint line on an old map turned blue, and
for the first time in seventy years

salmon returned to speckle the clear water
with spawning. I'd say that settles
the rivalry

between where we do and do not belong.
Listen to me chatter in relocated language,
then pour myself

into the dry stream before I spill over.
On this shore, even willows
rusting the banks speak, even the path

harlequinned with fallen leaves.
Seeds gather between my fingers.
Small wings in grass, they scatter.

Refugia (7)

A wolf emerges for the first time in a century
on the edge of a grassland.

A wolf disappears into a bison carcass,

caverned
       by its feast.

We look for the lost valley
where tiny resurrections meander.

The world hung on a skeleton made of physics—
each bone caught between the predator's gnashing teeth.

I could draw you a detailed model

of my *life environment.*
The seasons spangled into my skin

the way theories dissolve into uncertainty.

Every petal blossomed and blown,
then caught in my net,

a supplicant folded at the pew.

Fall Reckoning

You say these glowing trees
      are a lantern to see November by—

its hanging strings and thin places
held up to the light and exposed.

We wrap ourselves in the afternoon's weave
and cloak,

        its tangled overgrowth
a catalog of the late season's ripeness:

     dried berries on the stem
like outstretched palms,
       so open and indifferent.

We cross the threadbare mountain
wearing regret on our shoulders like tattered coats.

The forest shivers,

aspen leaves loosened until they glaze
      the dark path that led us here in gold.

When We Gathered to Stock Up On Light

We dipped two hundred candles
that day in late fall,

the box elders gone bright
over the garden

and we gone to wool shawls
and each other.

Wicks ready, our hands
pass them forward and back, then down

into kettles of honey-scented wax.
The thin strands grow

until they bear the sunlight
beaming through the last leaves,

bear the fire, hot beneath the wax,
bear the whole order of stars

shifting as we tilt into winter.
Bees settle on the drying rack,

move between our hands
as we lift and dip, hang and lift.

We did not sing, but were a song,
Hestia humming from her place

beside the cookpot,
stirring with a wooden spoon:

Here, take this beauty
and be warm.

Cusp with Various Visitations

In bowls, quince scent the morning
with membrillo and pie.
My thoughts sing, but written they fail
to leap forward—perhaps not knowing
would be a strategy less complicit
with hubris. *Elision* is the narrator's
last attempt to set it right, *eleison*
what happens when we fail.
The quince, green-gold and mottled,
were gleaned in Socorro by a woman
who tends her frail father on Sundays.
Today perches between tides:
one hand called autumn's last harvest,
one hand called winter's first fruit.
I prowl the kitchen, the page, the forest.
I don't set traps. What I thought
this was about is secondary
to what I sensed. The periphery
zigzags toward me while I wait.

Our Names Unfurl Across Winter

I.

Under the bare-branched tree,
my father lights a hand-rolled smoke,

jangles his cup of bones. Hush! I scold.
Tomorrow, ice will hinge the door.

At last, the fire will be lit. Ash and black
and warm. My firstborn wants to know

Persephone's original name,
wants to know which flowers

grew in the field where she danced,
why her mother spends winter in tears.

Wind breaks against fence rails,
the wood gone to splintered gray.

2.

Tomorrow, the geometry of the unseen
—an actual field—
will be up for discussion. Look closely
at the fabric
of our days, and you will see the careful seams
of my needle.
You will see my father (his long white hair,
his white beard)
pluck meteors from the desert's skin.
Not metaphor,
meteor. It is necessary to use the right name.
Like a Shabbat
that begins and ends at nightfall,
the new year
opens its hungry mouth just as the windows
are drawn
against darkness. Take me, winter morning,
to feed
the ghosts their bits and crumbs.
Scatter
bread. Let them rattle as they feast.

3.
His stories needle, an unrelenting
            wind. Ice skins morning,
feathers windows.
            When my hair is white, I will look
like him for the second time.

My daughter
            wakes in the dark, reads
                        the seams in my palm
            with small fingers.
Her face versus the past:
            leap and meteoric rise.

                        Small remembrance
drawn from the Lethe,
                        its crystal teeth snapping
            at the ankles of those crossing.

Submerged,
            the hungry and their quarrels quiet.
Names unspool
            from torn scrolls.

4.

What I say to my firstborn
is this: *Persephone's mother*
walked and wailed the fields
into fallow waiting, her tears
a scroll like grass is a scroll
of crickets and their cries,
like wind is a scroll of crossing
geese, high and honking on the day
the first snow fell, years ago
when I was small and you were
yet before me. A day of feathers
drifting into my palms. My father's
hair black. My mother's hair black.
The dark river biting at our backs.

Refugia (8)

After her birthday, my seven-year-old notices
        her sparkling pink balloon

sinking day by day a little lower.
   One night near the end, balloon floating at her ankles,
she sobs her revelation.

She knows she will wake
        to scraps on the floor:
                deflated Mylar shining on a string.

                As she sleeps I almost drive back to
   the dollar store
where boys huff helium in the wind.

           Imagine the beautiful deceit
of life evermore: Balloony fat again, bumping

the ceiling, a new ribbon curled in my child's hand.
What I would give to switch this and every loss,

         even when the remains have transfigured
            into their own

      unexpected beauty, even if, in the morning,

she will be ready to love whatever
ruin they have become.

Further Phrases in the Original Unspoken

Through fevers we decant the sun's
long leaving,
                        the cold gray evening
that petals into pink as gunshots

crack the mesa and a truck sputters
over Tetilla Peak's far flank.

Every drooping seed on every grama stem
sways within a mandorla. The sun

sets on the southern end of west,
and at dawn, frost will salt

the wooden footbridge.

I wander through disagreements
and other tight straits,

            braid and unbraid my hair,

accede to the trifecta we make
around the table—
                        demand, request, treaty.

I wear a mask framed in thorns.

We leave the lights off. Our lamps
unlit, our wings folded.

Omega

Astronomers sift density parameters into sickle and sigil,

craft circles around ascending stars.
Each conversation a hard freeze

on the moon's sparkling skin.

It's like a snowflake, fourth graders sigh as one by one
they telescope the distance

from desert floor to desert floor.
There are places that really do glitter.

I claim each node and mark it with my latitude, that origin,

that dark sky pouring in.
Omega already here: it keeps us in place.

Convergence simple—cosmology
can be tasted only after it is felt:

vinegar bright on the tongue, then delicious.

Archipelago with Ancestral Bodies
and Unnamed Landmarks of the Present

I.

I map the scattered archipelago's
rock and green-topped fragments:

one island for each of the faces
I can trace to the file and fold

of our family.
Here on the faded flyleaf

is another name I don't know,
a century-old missive harbored

in the cursive past.
Legends and letters confirm it:

prayers made a century ago still reach us.
Islands rise like spikes of red amaranth,

the haphazard sowing of black seed
across unprepared ground.

2.

     Scattered islands—

Obscured eyes look out
through my own.

I make a veil of old letters
     and handkerchiefs,

dress my daughter
in its kind and angled face.

In the closet's far reaches
there is plenty

of jaundiced lace and silk.

3.
My grandmother is at the market.

Her hunger
wears a blue jacket.

We rake our crumbs
into bowls.

They are perfect
if only for asking us to eat.

We answer with lips and fingers,
walk home together

past gardens gleaned
save for greenblack tomato stems
bearing frostbitten fruit.

We are neighbors,
but won't always be.

4.
One records the names of birds her children will not know;

One wants to marry but not be a stepmother;

One says, thank you for listening to me
        keen with my words;

One adds, it is the finality that is so hard;

One waits for hummingbirds to bring messages;

One can only wonder at the line she tries to draw,
        insistent in its wavering across the page.

5.
Every midnight our daughter slips
into our bed. We clasp her foot

or stray braid in cupped hands.

Though a neighbor's illuminated cross
blazes on the hillside, darkness

surrounds the apple tree.

Raccoons march the fence,
lit by the red tip of a cigarette.

All the next day, piñon jays take to task
the space between frozen ground

and tree tops. We eat lentils
on plain rice for dinner,

take holy books from their high shelf,
cover our heads with rags.

6.
Belief is no business of the young,
who can pretend anything.

Take the gown I dress in—

    lather
of soap root over earth-caked skin.

Each generation's circumference a land
eroded by sea.

        The boat was left adrift.

      You have never heard a call
like the one

sinking in these blue waters.

7.

Here you are, bones in bright hour

Here digit and palm, here grasp and hold

Here pelvis and clavicle, folded

Creature in the bower

Here breast and oaken slip

Here mist-settled grove

Here reckless and done

Are you here?

8.
I return after dark,
see the city in phosphorescent light—

how it stretches long arms
to gather up valley.

Of all the things to tell a child,
do not say she is too like her mother.

My grandmother wrote a letter, reckless
and done.

I heard her,

    Are you there?

slow on the stairs before dawn

9.
What do you want?
> First light and waking. The untilled scars of my face.

What will you do with the apples?
> My body aching in its cornices.

What did you inherit?
> Blindfold, and the sting of light when lifted.

Is it passing down?
> They call for us when we alone our dreams.

Have you named your child?
> Sweet berry on thorn bush.

Have you been back since the bright pollen month?
> As if I wanted secrets to fill my throat with tarred light.

What will you remember?
> Our names in the prayer book, five generations ago.

Is the tree half dead?
> Birds feasting on fruit.

Refugia (9)

The doves whisper me awake,

          my apple tree

      as widespread as mortal leaves can be.

      Each leaf an inflorescence,

          a conductor carrying heat.

O, pre-dawn

      water potential, how I do fear your

          reduction,

that and the limbs you will take with you.

      At sunrise, I pull curtains aside to watch

      the sky hemorrhage,

      call my child a foul name

because she called her sister

the same and that is conduction,

                                        the threshold
                    I force myself to bear. Who has studied

                                    our survival and can tell me when this
        degree
                                        of tension will decrease?

                    The tree doctor says the only way to make an old apple
            tree new
                                is to cut it to a stump

and watch it return a sapling.

As for the child,
                                I take her in my arms.

Nestle her against my belly,

                            where she still fits.

Waveform

Papi says the two lines
of our ancestry are twins

walking hand in hand
             backward
to one beautiful name.

He takes skewers of meat from the fire,
             hands me an iron key.

If prayer is an echo, how does it bend
into the reaches of our bodies,

ready-made, as they are, to listen?

The key slips into its lock
as late summer turns the berries,

elder and bane, into dark red drops.

If it is certainty you are looking for,
tend the water boiling in the cookpot.

Move it off the flame.

Origin of the Apple

"The center of origin is where the greatest diversity occurs . . . At Almaty, I could see with my own eyes the origin of the apple."

—Nikolai Vavilov

I.
Every family is a mountain
nooked with hollows.

Variations of trunks, twisted and rising on the long slope.

    Bud and bloom, pip
and slowly ripened fruit.

Deep in crested ridges,
        the first two become the rest.

2.

If I could trace this body back far enough
              through teasel beds and clear-cut meadows
I would be home.

Familiar to the people who look up in surprise
         at the stranger who wears their face.

Who carried a bucket
              —it must be milk—
across the fields to their table.

3.
I am sometimes religious,
but I do not know if it is god I believe in, or apples,

or if there is any difference.

I look at this forest, even in its falling,
and am brought to my knees.

4.
Here is origin: fruit on the mountain.

Where god created the apple,
the apple can be anything.

It is what color it chooses,
what flavor it wants,

wife to whichever wandering bee
with pollen-dusted feet it pleases.

Every star-seeded apple ever set on your plate
was born from this place.

5.
Every thread
        you unravel
from your dress

splits in its threshing,

each ancestor whose name you learn
is undone before you reach
        her face.

You will never know the feast
from which you were born.

Right of First Refugium

If you cannot find a Snowdon lily
in Snowdonia, try the alplily

close to home, try singing *Oriri, oriri*
all winter. First frost

is not on the list of flowers with no smell,
but thrums cold, flagrant in my hand all the same—

Not fragrance, though it surrounds,
and not the exact name for loss, but something similar.

Women bare swells named breast, named belly,
that refugium that survives demolition birth after birth.

Make me a figure with a womb
and relict heart. Make me

the seam that holds tattered land together
and let me be the speaker that sings

> *rise, rise*

all across this shapely ground.

Acknowledgments

About Place Journal: "Landscape with Santa Fe River Restored to Its Historic Channel After 100 Years"

Anomaly: "The Washerwoman Maps Her Body Before Death"

Boston Review: "Dear Future Child"

Heron Tree: "Equinox"

Interim: "The Ashram at Leigh Mill Road"; "The Trouble with Belief"; "Phrases in the Original Unspoken"; "Refugia (4), (5), (7)"

Kenyon Review Online: "For the Record"; "Our Names Unfurl Across Winter"

Raven Chronicle: "Origin of the Apple"

Sonora Review: "The Carp Pond"

Taos Journal of Poetry: "Message in a Bottle from the Sea of Cortez"

Taproot: "When We Gathered to Stock Up on Light"

Terrain.org: "The Trouble with Belief"; "The Tree Coroners"; "Dowsing"

The Hopper: "Grass Widow"

Thank you to Claudia Keelan, Donald Revell, Ronaldo Wilson, and Sasha Steenson for selecting this book for the Test Site Poetry Series. I am so grateful.

Thank you to Alrica Goldstein, Sara Hendricksen, and the University of Nevada Press for bringing *Refugia* into the world.

Thank you to my teachers Sherwin Bitsui, Joan Naviyuk Kane, Santee Frazier, Rachel Eliza Griffiths, and James Thomas Stevens. So much was rearranged inside me while studying with you.

Thank you to my IAIA cohort, especially Beatrice Szymkowiak who helped with early drafts of this manuscript.

Thank you to Maggie Smith who has a special knack for shuffling the deck just so.

Thank you to Jennifer Ferraro, Barbara Rockman, Ginger Legato, Sharon Franklet, Monique Sanchez, Kim Parko, Anne Haven McDonnell, and Stella Reed, for the conversations, feedback, and inspiration that sustained me while writing *Refugia*.

Elliot Ryan, in so many ways you have honored my voice. The life we share permeates these pages, and your love is this book's scaffolding. Thank you.

Thank you to Grandma Rose, to my parents, Lia and Lorenzo Bello, and my daughters, Cora and Maida. I am so honored to be the bridge between your lives. This book is dedicated to you, and to the ones who come after us.

Notes

The epigraph by Chase Twichell is excerpted with permission from her poem "Touch-me-not," included in *Horses Where the Answers Should Have Been: New and Selected Poems.*

Robert DeWitt Ivey wrote and illustrated *Flowering Plants of New Mexico,* which is referenced in "Guide to Flowering Plants." Michael Moore, who appears smoking Nat Shermans, authored *Medicinal Plants of the Mountain West* among other essential guides, and directed the Southwest School of Botanical Medicine.

"The Tree Coroners" borrows its title from an article of the same name in *High Country News* (*High Country News,* Dec. 16, 2013).

"Grail Story" draws from Wolfram Von Eschenbach's medieval epic *Parzival.*

"Grass Widow" takes the phrase "I am full of babies" from the poem "[Summa Mathematica]" by Leslie Harrison.

"Notes for Future Botanists" borrows Lucie Brock-Broido's line, "in the finished world / I will be wind-awry."

"Solar Pinholes" is after Arthur Sze.

"The Carp Pond" is dedicated to Cara Esquibel.

"Origin of the Apple" takes its epigraph from Gary Paul Nabhan's essay about the Russian botanist Nikolai Vavilov and his journey to Almaty, "The Fatherland of Apples," in *Orion Magazine*'s May/ June 2008 issue.

The "Refugia" sequence draws upon fragments and ideas gleaned from a number of scientific papers on refugia and climate change, especially "Managing Climate Change Refugia for Climate Adaptation" by Toni Lynn Morelli et al., "Microrefugia" by Valentí Rull, and "Refugia revisited" by John R Stewart et al.

About the Author

Kyce Bello is the inaugural winner of the Test Site Poetry Series. Her poems have appeared in *Boston Review, Interim, Kenyon Review Online, Sonora Review, Terrain.org, Taos Journal of Poetry, The Wayfarer*, and *Anomaly*, among other publications. She received her MFA from the Institute of American Indian Arts, and lives with her family in Santa Fe, New Mexico. *Refugia* is her first book.